Images of Wrexham

The County Borough through the camera lens

Geoffrey A. Jones

With a commentary by

W. Alister Williams

Images of Wrexham – the County Borough through the camera lens
first published in Wales in 2007 by
Bridge Books
61 Park Avenue
Wrexham
LL12 7AW

A full on-line catalogue is available at:
www.bridgebooks.co.uk

ISBN 978-1-84494-038-7

A CIP record of this book is available from the British Library

Set in Gill Sans

Printed and bound in China by CTPS

To

Christopher, Clare and Rebecca

Introduction

Images of Wrexham, the County Borough through the camera lens, is a totally new collection of photographs which have never previously been published, all taken by local photographer, Geoffrey Jones. They show the area through its landscapes and buildings. During my years of gathering and publishing old photographs of Wrexham, I have never come across such a unique collection of beautiful images that capture the essence of Wrexham County Borough. I feel certain that, in years to come, many of these photographs will become definitive images.

Apart from the obvious link of all the photographs relating to the County Borough of Wrexham, an underlying theme of this collection is that everything changes. The town of Wrexham has undergone a lengthy metamorphosis and is now emerging from its cocoon with a very different identity from that which it had twenty-five years ago. This has meant the loss of many familiar townscapes and buildings, some of which will be greatly missed. Much of what has gone was perhaps viewed through rose-tinted glasses and does not really deserve to be missed. Some new developments have worked well, enhancing the town and making it a more pleasant place in which to live and work. Others are great losses to the heritage of the area, although most of the buildings which fit into this category disappeared as long ago as the 1940s (the Town Hall) and the 1960s (the Gatehouse in Priory Street). This process of change has not ended and as this book goes to print there are still massive redevelopment projects ongoing in the town; a future chronicler will have to decide their value in the overall scheme of Wrexham's redevelopment.

There have also been great changes outside of the town, mostly in the area covered by the old Wrexham Rural District Council. Here long-established heavy industries have declined and gone; some by natural process, others the result of political machinations. These changes have brought about the re-structuring and re-use of the landscape to cater for the economic world of the twenty-first century. Gone are the steel works, the coal mines, the limestone quarries, the brick works; and in their place has come the curiosity value of historical buildings, memorials to a vanished economic heritage. Many of these landscapes have altered to become valuable residential and leisure areas and it is becoming increasingly difficult to identify the old heavy-industrial landscapes.

Wrexham County Borough's geographical position makes it unique in Wales. Its eastern boundary runs along the border with England. The River Dee, one of the great rivers of Wales, which finishes its journey to the sea in England, is a daunting physical barrier which has had a marked effect upon the landscape and the people who inhabit the area. The river's flood plain has formed an area of rich, gently undulating agricultural land in the east of the County Borough. Further west, the land rises sharply into the Welsh hills and, to the south, the Berwyn

Mountains, areas of dense woodland, deep green valleys and isolated moors; beautiful to look at and a walker's paradise. It is an area that has certainly been blessed and remains almost unknown to people from outside of the area who rush through it on their way to the mountains of Snowdonia or to the beaches of mid and north Wales. Perhaps some of the photographs in this book will inspire people to get out and explore the beauty that is on their doorstep.

This is a book that is primarily about today and the future, but the captions to each photograph give a brief glimpse of the past. Without an understanding of yesterday's landscapes, it would be impossible to appreciate the environment of the twenty-first century.

W. Alister Williams
Wrexham, 2007

Image

Overleaf: **1.** *Acton Park, winter*
Acton Hall (which stood on the site of the modern apartment block overlooking Herbert Jennings Avenue) was home to the Jeffreys family from the sixteenth to the eighteenth centuries and the birthplace of George Jeffreys, 1st Baron Wem, better known to history as the notorious Judge Jeffreys. The estate was bought in 1785 by Sir Foster Cunliffe who laid out the parkland which forms the basis of the modern park. It remained the seat of the Cunliffe family until the beginning of the twentieth century when it was let to Sir William Hope Nelson and then sold in 1917.

Left: **2.** *Acton Park*
Acton Park, a green lung in the centre of Wrexham, has been open to the public since the 1920s when it was bought by local businessman William Aston who eventually sold it to the Borough of Wrexham.

A substantial area of the present-day park was laid out as smallholdings for ex-servicemen after the First World War. The house named The Holding at the eastern end of the park, close to Tapley Avenue, is a surviving example of one of the eleven smallholding houses that were scattered around the estate.

Left: **3.** *Acton Gates, Chester Road*
The main entrance to the old Acton Park estate, this gateway was erected in 1820 to a design by the Chester-based architect, Thomas Harrison. The four ornamental greyhounds are the crest on the arms of the Cunliffe family, owners of Acton Park from 1785–1917. The mid-nineteenth century lodge, built for Sir Robert Cunliffe, 5th Baronet, can be seen in the background.

Facing: **4.** *Eisteddfod Stones, Acton Park*
The stone circle, laid out for the 1933 National Eisteddfod of Wales, was originally sited at Bodhyfryd (the site of the present-day police station) before being moved here as part of William Aston's rock garden and used for the 1977 National Eisteddfod.

WESTMINSTER DRIVE
RHODFA SAN STEFFAN

Facing: **5.** *Park Avenue, spring*
Park Avenue was laid out between c.1910 and the 1930s. it was originally known as Cooper's Lane, after Joseph Cooper of Bodhyfryd. In the 1920s, proposals were made by Liverpool architects Lockwood, Abercrombie and Saxon that Park Avenue should curve from approximately the junction with Westminster Drive and go across the Nine Acre Field to link into Chester Road at the junction of Rhosnesni Lane and Price's Lane. The plan was rejected and the present line of the road was adopted and plots sold to private builders. WBC built fourteen 'semi-detached villas' (nos. 90–116) to accommodate key workers. The name was changed to Park Avenue in 1932.

Above: **6.** *The Law Courts, Bodhyfryd*
Wrexham's Magistrates' Courts were originally located in the old Town Hall at the top of Town Hill before moving to the County Buildings on Regent Street. They were moved into this purpose-built building on Bodhyfryd in 1978.

Right: **7.** *Waterworld*
Waterworld, one of Wrexham's most striking buildings, was built as the town's swimming baths and opened in 1970. Its most unusual feature is the parabolic roof. The building underwent a major refurbishment and re-design in the 1990s and was opened as Waterworld by HM The Queen in 1998.

Facing: **8.** *The Royal Welch Fusiliers War Memorial, Bodhyfryd*

This emotive statue, one of the finest pieces of sculpture to emerge from the post-Great War flood of war memorial art, depicts a Royal Welchman of the eighteenth century passing the Colours on to his twentieth century successor. Specially commissioned from the noted sculptor, Sir Goscombe John, the memorial was originally located at the junction of Regent Street and Grosvenor Road before being moved to its present location during the 1960s.

Right: **9.** *The Arc, Lord Street*

The Arc was commissioned by Wrexham Maelor Borough Council from the Scottish sculptor David Annand as a commemorative statue for the coal and steel industries which played such a prominent role in the area's history. It was unveiled in 1996. The figure nearest the camera in the photograph represents a steel worker and the one furthest away a coal miner. At the base of the statue is a short poem by Crowned Eisteddfod Bard Merddyn ap Dafydd.

Y Bwa
Uwch y waedd, drwy'r gawod chwys — a helynt
Y morthwylion stormus,
Heibio'r awr sy'n bwyta brys,
Mae tynfa yma at enfys.

The Arc
Above the cry, through streaming sweat — and the storm
Of angry hammers,
Past the hour that devours haste,
We are drawn towards rainbows.

Left: 10. *Grosvenor Road*
Wrexham is a town that has undergone considerable changes, particularly during the last twenty-five years. Today, as the town emerges in its modern guise, it displays a pleasing mix of traditional and mod architecture with new, purpose-built features and successful adaptations of buildings that have been pa of the local townscape for many years.

The steel and glass link between two traditional brick-built houses in Grosvenor Road has worked we both practically (as offices for a legal firm) and aesthetically.

Above: 11. *Rhosddu Road*
Originally Turners ironmongery store, this building on the corner of Lord Street and Rhosddu Road became the Wrexham premises of Tesco. After a major redevelopment in the 1990s, when the whole building was clad in brick, it forms a striking feature in the town centre.

Facing: 12. *The Guildhall and Coronation Walk*
Wrexham Borough Council bought Llwyn Isaf, the former Vicarage in 1951 and built a new Guildhall o the site which opened in 1961, replacing the old Guildhall on Chester Street. With the creation of Wrexham Maelor Borough Council in 1974 this building also accommodated the staff of the former Wrexham Rural District Council. Coronation Walk commemorates the visit of HM The Queen and HF Prince Philip during their Coronation Tour of 1953.

ng : **13.** *The Old Library, Queen Square*
ened in 1907, this purpose-built public library
; the gift of the Scottish-American
anthropist Andrew Carnegie. It served as the
n library and museum until 1973 when the
v Library and Arts Centre was opened on
yn Isaf. Today the building houses Wrexham
C's computer department.

nt: **14.** *Guildhall Offices, Lambpit Street.*
e of Wrexham's oldest streets, Lambpit Street,
demolished (along with the Vegetable Market
part of Queen Street) in the early 1990s and
new building was opened in 1992. The
ical-topped spire replicates a similar tower
ch stood opposite on the corner of the
etable Market building. At the rear of this
ding (on the site of the present-day Guildhall
park) stood the Glynn Cinema.

35

acing: **15.** *The Doors of Wrexham.*
. selection of doorways from the centre of Wrexham displayng the use of
·aditional building materials – wood, sandstone and brick.

ight: **16.** *The Butchers' Market, High Street..*
he neo-Tudor facade of the Victorian Butchers' Market was designed by local
·chitect Thomas Penson and built by the Wrexham Market Hall Company on the
te of the Oak and the Bear public houses. It was opened in 1848. The bay-
·indowed room on the first floor accommodated the market offices. This was the
·st of Wrexham's three indoor markets (the others being the Vegetable Market
nd the Butter Market). Previously, the town's butchers had occupied stalls in High
treet, Church Street and Abbot Street.

The Beach
LLOYDS BAR
LLOYDS Nº1 BAR
WYNNSTAY ARMS HOTEL

Facing: **17.** *High Street*

Once the commercial heart of Wrexham, High Street has undergone enormous changes during the past ten years, and has been described as the centre of the town's 'wining and dining' area. The development of the Eagles Meadow will result in this street again becoming a major pedestrian thoroughfare into the town centre.

The Wynnstay Arms Hotel has occupied this prominent site since at least the early years of the eighteenth century (when it was known as The George). In 1723 it was greatly enlarged and the name changed to The Eagles (or The Three Spread Eagles), being a reference to the arms of the Williams Wynn family of Wynnstay Hall, Ruabon. It was at this time that the open ground at the rear of the hotel took on the name Eagles Meadow. By the nineteenth century the name had again changed to the Wynnstay Arms. A plaque on the front of the hotel records that it was here that the Football Association of Wales was formed in 1876.

A walk along High Street and Town Hill will reveal examples of every type of architectural style from 1700 to the late twentieth century. Remarkably, most of these buildings blend well with each other to form one of the most attractive streets in the town.

Above: **18.** *Yorke Street*

Once a fairly narrow street lined with small shops, public houses and tenement houses, Yorke Street underwent major changes during the 1960s when the western side was demolished to produce an open vista of the Parish Church. The name of the street was originally Marchnad y Moch (Swine Market) then became known as the Street Below the Church (or the Street Below the Eagles) before becoming Yorke Street during the nineteenth century. The Welsh translation of Yorke Street as Stryt Efrog makes no sense and should perhaps be changed to the ancient Marchnad y Moch.

ıcing: **19.** *The Parish Church of St Giles*
ndoubtedly the jewel in Wrexham's architectural crown, e Parish Church has dominated the town centre since it as built at the end of the fifteenth century. The present ıilding is probably the third church to have been built (the st being probably on a site very close to the eastern end the Island Green Retail Park.

1463 the tower of the second church was destroyed by e and, as a consequence, the greater part of the church as then rebuilt. The tower and the chancel were added in e early 1500s. There is circumstantial evidence to support e claim that the rebuilding of the church was funded by argaret Beaufort, Countess of Derby, the mother of King enry VII. In the mid-sixteenth century attempts were ade to make the Parish Church the centre of the diocese stead of St Asaph.

ght: **20.** *Parish Church Gates and Church Street*
he beautiful wrought iron gates were produced by obert Davies of Croesfoel Smithy, Wrexham and erected 1720. Originally positioned further into Church Street vhere they were attached to the buildings on either side) ey were moved to their present position in 1820.

hurch Street is one of the oldest streets in the town and os 7–10, originally a medieval hall house with a timber uck frame, is possibly the oldest building in Wrexham and ay pre-date the Parish Church by 100–150 years.

he shops which can be seen here date from the eventeenth century, with eighteenth century additions.

Facing: 21. *The Churchyard and Temple Row, winter*
Amongst the notable people buried here are: Elihu Yale of Plas Grono (benefactor of Yale Univesity in New England); Sir Roger Palmer of Cefn Park (survivor of the Charge of the Light Brigade); John Downman (artist and Royal Academician) and Robert Davies (smith who produced the churchyard gates).

Above: 22. *The Tomb of Elihu Yale*

Below: 23. *Yale University Stone*
A replica of the tower of Wrexham's Parish Church was built at Yale University and one stone was taken from Wrexham and placed in the structure in America in 1918.

Left: 24. *Parish Church Tower*
The tower, one of the famed 'Seven Wonders of Wales' stands 45m (147ft) high and is made of soft sandstone. This highly decorated structure has suffered badly from the action of weathering and pollution. Many of the features on the tower appear to be a celebration of the Tudor dynasty of monarchs and of King Henry VIII in particular.

Left: **25.** *Central Arcade, Hope Street*
Built in 1891, on a site that had once been the King's Head public house, by the Wrexham Arcade Company, it provided eighteen attractive lock-up shops, offices and a photographic studio.

Below: **26.** *Overton Arcade*
This arcade was built in 1868 and named after the Overton family who owned the site. Originally providing small shop premises, the arcade fell into decline and, in the latter part of the twentieth century, many of the shops were absorbed into the adjoining High Street premises. During the 1980s, the arcade was restored, recreating the Victorian atmosphere.

Above: **27.** *Henblas Street*

One of the more recent shopping developments in the town centre, Henblas Street now accommodates a variety of local and national retailers. Historically, Wrexham was always a significant market town serving a large hinterland, but, during the twentieth century, struggled to compete with the nearby city of Chester. A concerted effort by various authorities over the past twenty-five years has led to a renaissance of the town as a shopping centre, a process which continues apace with the Eagles Meadow development.

Henblas Street took its name from the Hen Blas (Old Hall) which stood on Queen Street. The north side of the street was re-developed between the 1870s and 1890s when the large indoor Vegetable Market was built there. The whole site between Henblas Street and Lambpit Street was cleared during the 1980s and the present-day shopping development opened in the late 1990s.

Above and right: **28, 29 & 30.** *Charles Street*
According to the historian Alfred Palmer, this street was known as Beast Market Street until the late eighteenth century. It comprises a number of interesting and historic buildings, including several that are timber-framed and still contain wattle and daub infills. No 15 (which dates back to at least 1650), was the birthplace of the cleric and academic, Dr Jonathan Edwards, who became Principal of Jesus College, Oxford in 1686 and Vice-Chancellor of Oxford University. The three-storey building on the left of photograph 28 was designed and built by noted local architect Thomas Penson. The last public house in the street, the Elephant and Castle (see picture 28), closed in *c.*1999.

Facing: **31.** *Wrexham Museum, Regent Street*
Designed by Thomas Penson as a barracks for the local militia, this building was opened in 1857. After only twenty years, new barracks were built in Hightown and the Regent Street building was converted for use as the Court of Petty Sessions (Magistrates Court) and Police Headquarters. The police moved from here to their new headquarters in 1976 and the courts moved out in 1978. After a short period as the Art Department of Aston College, it became the Wrexham County Borough Museum in 1996.

wrexham
wrecsam
Museum
wrexham
wrecsam
Amgueddfa
No 2 COURT

Left: **32.** *St Mary's Cathedral, Regent Street*
Following the Reformation of the mid-sixteenth century, the Roman Catholic Church had no place of worship in Wrexham until St David's RC Chapel was built in King Street following the passing of the Catholic Emancipation Act in 1829. Local industrialist, Richard Thompson of Stansty Hall, paid for the building of this neo-Gothic Cathedral Church of Our Lady of Sorrows as a memorial to his wife, Ellen. Designed by Edward Pugin (the son of the renowned Gothic revivalist architect Augustus Pugin) it became the Pro-Cathedral for the newly formed Diocese of Menevia in 1907. In 1987, it became the cathedral church of the Diocese of Wrexham.

Facing: **33.** *The Parciau (Belle Vue Park)*
Originally part of the Wynnstay estate, plans were first put forward to convert this area into a municipal park in about 1876. Two years later, part of it was developed as a gravel pit. In 1907 it was sold to Wrexham Borough Council and laid out as a formal park to designs prepared by J. Cheal & Sons of Westminster. The bandstand was erected in 1914. The Parciau was the site of the 1933 National Eisteddfod of Wales.

Left: **34.** *Statue of Queen Victoria, The Parciau*
Commissioned by Wrexham Borough Council to commemorate the reign of Queen Victoria, this statue was sculpted by Henry Price, a former student of the Wrexham College of Art who had already been commissioned to produce a bronze statue of the Queen for the parade ground at Aldershot. The Wrexham statue was a duplicate of this. It was unveiled in 1905 and stood in front of the Guildhall in Chester Street until that area was cleared for redevelopment and it was moved to its present site.

Above: **35.** *The Parciau*

Right: **36.** *Wrexham Cemetery, Ruabon Road*
This site was almost certainly used for industrial purposes (perhaps as a clay or gravel pit) until its purchase in 1874 when it was laid out as a new cemetery and recreational facility by local horticulturalist Yeoman Strachen. The cemetery was officially opened in 1876 and has since been expanded twice. The clever use of the gradient of the land, ornamental trees and meandering footpaths and complete with specially-designed chapels and a lodge, it was regarded as one of the major attractive features of the town at the end of the nineteenth century. This view shows the Roman Catholic section looking from the Bersham Road entrance towards the Cemetery Chapel. The large grave on the left is that of John Beirne, a leading local businessman and politician (Mayor of Wrexham in 1876).

PRAY FOR THE SOUL OF
ALEXANDER BEIRNE
AGED 27 YEARS
MAY HE REST IN PEACE

Left: **37.** *Free Polish Forces Memorial, Wrexham Cemetery*
Wrexham Cemetery is an official Commonwealth War Graves Cemetery containing many graves from the Second World War, a large proportion of which are to members of the Free Polish Forces who served with the British Armed Forces. The location of the Polish Hospital at Penley after the war meant that the town maintained its association with the Polish community and, as a consequence, this memorial was erected in Wrexham Cemetery.

Above: **38 & 39.** *River Gwenfro, Maelor Hospital*
Once a major feature of the town, the River Gwenfro flowed through Croesnewydd, Watery Road, Brook Street, Rivulet Road and The Dunks before eventually joining the River Clywedog at King's Mills. Culverting during the nineteenth century led to the river all but disappearing until decisions were made to feature it in several of the more modern redevelopments. In photograph 38 the river flows under the bridge which links the new Maelor Hospital buildings to the old Maelor General Hospital buildings. In photograph 39, the river forms a calming background to the accommodation for the Shooting Star Cancer Unit at the Maelor Hospital.

MSI

Overleaf and left: **40 & 41.** *Croesnewydd Hall*

An often forgotten architectural gem is Croesnewydd Hall, the house built by Peter Ellice in c.1696. It was the home of Miss Mary Myddelton from 1719 until her death in 1747 and later passed into the ownership of the Fitzhugh family of Plas Power. The house was bought by Clwyd County Council in 1984 and was extensively restored as the focal building in the Croesnewydd Technology Park development.

Below and facing: **42 & 43.** *Yale College Wrexham*

Wrexham's further education provision is found at Yale College Wrexham, partly housed in the former Wrexham & East Denbighshire Memorial Hospital (built after the First World War in memory of the local men who had lost their lives in the conflict), the old Grove Park Grammar School and the new buildings which link the two. Today, it caters for over 12,000 students.

WREXHAM & EAST DENBIGHSHIRE MEMORIAL HOSPITAL
1914 - 1918

Left: **44, 45, 46, 47 & 48.** *Memorial plaques*
Various memorial plaques commemorating notable citizens of Wrexham:
44. — Edwin Hughes, the last survivor of the Charge of the Light Brigade. Mount Street.
45. — John Godfrey Parry-Thomas, holder of the World Land Speed Record. 6 Spring Road, Rhosddu.
46. — David Samuel Anthony Lord, recipient of the Victoria Cross, 1944. 15 Cilcen Grove, Acton.
47. — Alfred Neobard Palmer, local historian. Inglenook, Bersham Road.
48. — William Low, Channel Tunnel pioneer. Grove Park Road.

Facing: **49.** *Trinity Presbyterian Church, King Street*
Built of striking red Ruabon bricks, to a design by W. Beddoe Rees of Cardiff, this church was opened in 1907. The large window is decorated with Art Nouveau-style tracery.

CAUTION
SKY

Above and left: 50 & 51. *The Racecourse, Mold Road*
Originally laid out as a horse-racing course for the Wrexham Yeomanry Cavalry in 1807, part of the ground became used by the Wrexham Football and Wrexham Cricket Clubs during the latter part of the nineteenth century (the first football match being played here in 1872). Since 1887, Wrexham AFC have always played their home games here.

Facing, top left: 52. *The Turf Hotel, Mold Road*
The name of this public house is a reminder of the origins of the football ground. Today, it is the only public house inside the grounds of a British football league club.

Facing, right: 53. *Island Green Brewery*
Wrexham was once known as 'the Burton-on-Trent of Wales' with numerous breweries, both large and small, located in the town centre. Today, they are all gone and all that remains are some brewery buildings that have been adapted for other use.

Facing, bottom left: 54. *Nag's Head, Mount Street*
Virtually all that remains of the Nag's Head Brewery, this building dates back to the early eighteenth century.

MARSTON'S
THE TURF
THE TURF
THE TURF
BAR SNACKS
DARTS POOL
ENTERTAINMENT
CAR PARK

NAGS HEAD
FOOD

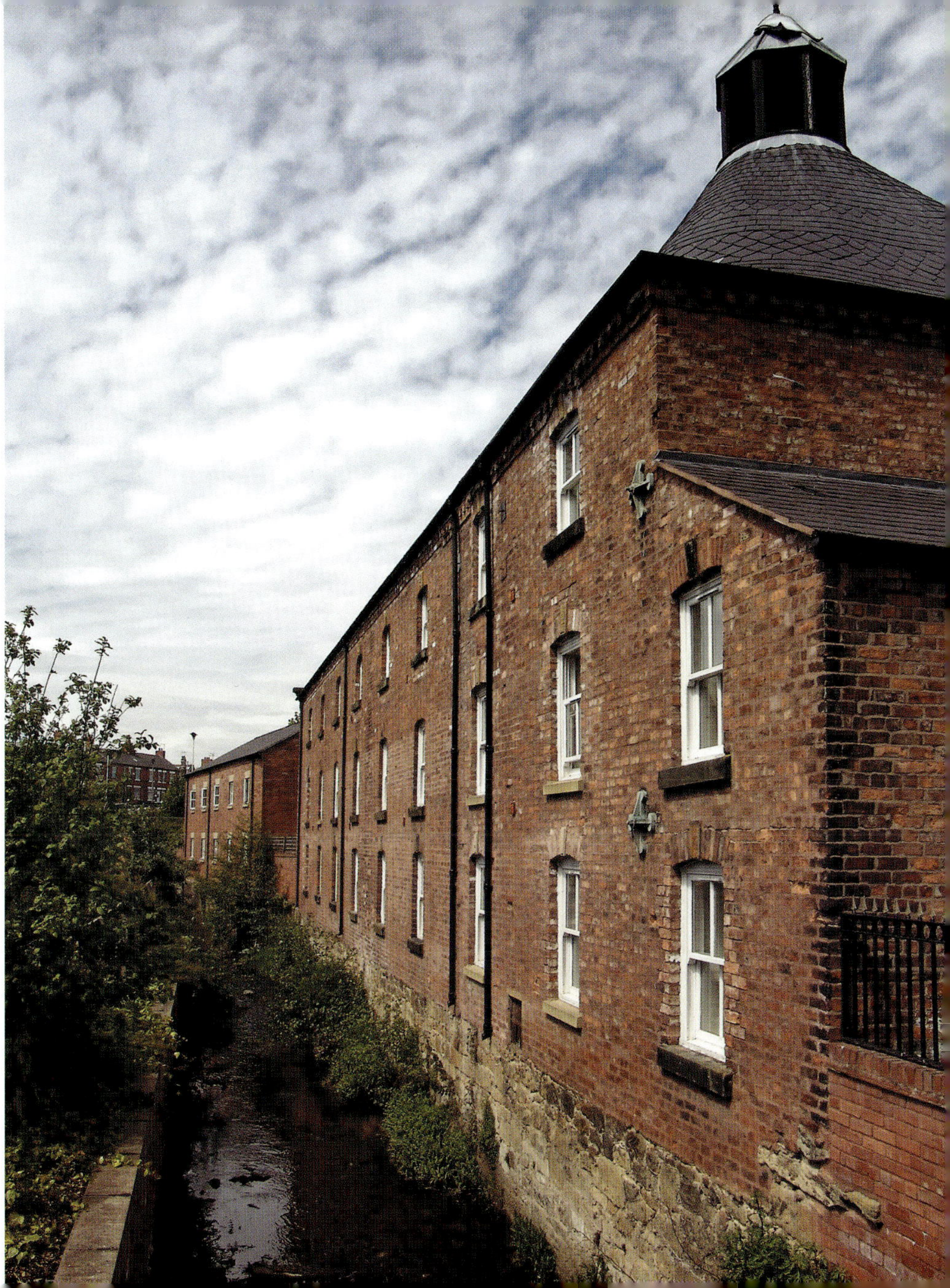

Welcome to a world of learning
NEWI
Aelod o Brifysgol Cymru · Member of the University of Wales

Facing and right: **55 & 56.** *North East Wales Institute, Plas Coch*
Wrexham has a record in education that goes back to the end of the sixteenth century when Wrexham Grammar School was founded. In the nineteenth century Wrexham made a bid to become the home of the proposed University College of North Wales but lost out to Bangor. By way of consolation, the Borough Council founded the Wrexham School of Science and Art, originally accommodated in Argyle Street before moving into the upper floor of the new fire station in Guildhall Square, Chester Street. It continued to serve the town and surrounding area until the Denbighshire Technical College opened in Regent Street in 1927. Within ten years it was realised that a major expansion was necessary to cope with the demand for places but all plans were put on hold following the outbreak of war in 1939. A thirty-acre site was purchased on what had once been part of the old horse-racing track and work began in 1949. This building, designed by Saxon, Smith & Partners of Chester, was officially opened in 1953 and was awarded the RIBA architectural bronze medal by the Liverpool Architectural Society in 1957. It is regarded by many as a fine example of post-war British architecture and remains almost unchanged today.

The North-East Wales Institute was formed in September 1975 by combining the Denbighshire Technical College (which became known as Aston College), the Flintshire Technical College (Kelsterton College) and Cartrefle College (Wrexham) with the intention of becoming a higher education (HE) college. In 1993, NEWI became an incorporated college of higher education and all HE courses were centralised at the Plas Coch site by 1995 with FE (further education) courses being transferred to Yale College Wrexham and Deeside College. In 2004, NEWI became a full member of the University of Wales.

Left and above: **57 & 58.** *Wrexham General Station, Mold Road*
Wrexham's first railway station was built on this site by the Shrewsbury & Chester Railway to a desig by Thomas Penson. It was demolished in 1881 and the present station built by the Great Western Railway Company in a 'French chateau' style. The buildings have remained largely unchanged since that time and, following a major refurbishment in the 1980s, is now a wonderful example of a working, late nineteenth century, provincial railway station.

59. *Llwyn Onn, Cefn Road*
Perhaps nothing typifies the changes that have occurred in the countryside as much as the introduction of multi-coloured crops. Today, instead of living in 'a green and pleasant land' we are surrounded by fields of bright blues, purples and yellow, such as this crop of rape seed on Cefn Road.

Left: **60.** *JCB, Wrexham Industrial Estate*
Just to disprove the commonly held belief that all modern industry and employment is a blot on the landscape, many of the factories on the Wrexham Industrial Estate are designed to blend into their background and, if possible, enhance it. There is perhaps no better example of this than the JCB factory which was opened in 1998.

Facing: **61.** *Redwither Tower, Wrexham Industrial Estate*
In 1941 the Royal Ordnance Factory, Marchwiel began the production of propellants (nitroglycerine, nitrocellulose and tetryl nitrate) on a massive 1,730 acre site. The site employed 10,000 workers and was served by its own railway network which was linked to the national system at Marchwiel. The factory closed shortly after the end of the war and the site was adapted for use as an industrial estate. Today, many buildings from the wartime period have survived and can be seen scattered all around the entire area of the estate and some have been adapted for modern usage. A post-war building, the massive Redwither Tower, originally the power station for the estate, has been adapted by Wrexham Council for use by light industry and provides state-of-the-art conference and function facilities

Facing: **62.** *Holt Bridge*
This late medieval bridge spans the Dee on the border between Wales and England. There was once a tower and gatehouse, protected by a drawbridge above the third arch from the Welsh bank which was the scene of a minor battle in 1643 during the English Civil War.

Above: **63.** *Kenyon Hall, Holt*
Opened in 1892 and built on a site donated to the village by Lord Kenyon, this corrugated iron building has served the village well as a 'non-political and undenominational institution, used for all classes of meetings, and free to the people of Holt'. It was fully restored in the late 1990s.

Right: **64.** *The Cross, Holt*
The old medieval Cross in the square provides a focal point for the village.

Facing: **65.** *River Dee, Holt*
The view looking downstream. Located in the meadows to the west of the river was an important Roman works depot for the XX Legion at Chester. Excavations at the beginning of the twentieth century uncovered traces of several buildings and a number of kilns used for making clay tiles and pottery.

Above: **66.** *Holt Castle*
Little now remains of Holt Castle built by the Earl of Surrey at the end of the thirteenth century. Built of red sandstone, pentagonal in shape, with a tower at each corner, the castle was the control centre for the lordship of Bromfield and Yale. During the English Civil War it was held by the Crown until after the fall of Chester.

Right: **67.** *Parish Church, Holt*
St Chad's is one of a number of churches in north-east Wales rebuilt by the Stanley family in the late fifteenth century on a site where there has been a church since at least 1395.

Overleaf: **68.** *Trevalyn Hall, Rossett*
Undoubtedly the finest Elizabethan house in the county, Trevalyn Hall was built for John Trevor in c.1576. His son, Sir John Trevor, built Plas Teg, the Jacobean mansion near Pontblyddyn.

Facing: **72.** *Trevor Arms, Marford*
Dating from at least 1812, this was a significant inn on the main Chester–Wrexham route. The road originally went straight past the inn (through the trees visible in the background of the photograph) until a new road was built up Marford Hill. The building is part of the scheme carried out by John Boydell for the Trefalyn Hall Estate although the decoration is of a simpler style than that found on the nearby cottages (see photographs 70 & 71).

Overleaf: **69.** *Rossett Mill, Rossett*
Powered by water from the River Alyn, via an under-shot wheel, Rossett Mill was built in the mid-seventeenth century and was extended two hundred years later.

Above and right: **70 & 71.** *Trevalyn Estate Cottages, Marford*
The 'chocolate-box' style cottages at the foot of Marford Hill are unique and were built in the early nineteenth century for the Trevalyn Estate, probably at the instigation of the agent, John Boydell. Some of the cottages have what appear to be bayonets or pike-heads fitted as window bars which, according to local legend, were originally issued to repel any attacks by the Chartists in the 1840s.

TREVOR ARMS
HOTEL
HOTEL
RESTAURANT
PLAY AREAS

Facing: **73.** *Vicarage Gorse, Gresford*

Above: **74.** *Gresford Churchyard*

This churchyard, which completely surrounds the Parish Church, is of the traditional Welsh '*llan*' type (*llan* translating as the land on which a church stands and not, as is generally believed, the church itself). Before the construction of the turnpike road from Chester to Wrexham, the main road came along Gresford High Street, past the church and then turned right for Marford along the line of Pant Lane.

Right: **75.** *All Saints, Gresford*

Regarded as one of the finest parish churches in Wales, All Saints is in the Perpendicular style and was built in the late fifteenth century. The funding almost certainly came from Margaret Beaufort, Countess of Derby, wife of Thomas Stanley (as was the case with the parish churches at Wrexham and Holt). The peal of bells is listed as one of the 'Seven Wonders of Wales'.

acing: **76.** *Village Pond, Gresford*

ight and below: **77 & 78.** *Gresford Colliery Disaster Memorial, Pandy*

he Gresford Colliery Disaster occurred at 2 a.m. on 22 September 1934 in the Dennis Section of ne pit. This was the worst disaster in the North Wales Coalfield. The mine was closed for six nonths and production of coal resumed in the Martin Section in January 1936. Gresford Colliery ventually closed in 1974. This memorial uses the wheel from the Dennis headgear.

verleaf: **79.** *Pant-yr-Ochain, Gresford*

oday a popular pub/restaurant, the Pant-yr-Ochain has a history dating back to the early sixteenth entury and the present-day building still displays some very early Tudor timber and brickwork. It ter became the property of the Robinson family of Gwersyllt Hall and eventually passed to the Cunliffe family of Acton Hall in 1785. In 1835, it was extended and split into a farmhouse and a rivate residence for the unmarried daughters of Sir Foster Cunliffe. The small lake in front of the all and the larger Flash lake nearby are examples of kettle holes, formed during the last Ice Age.

ER COF
AM Y 266 O LOWYR A GOLLODD
EU BYWYDAU YN NHANCHWA
GWAITH GLO GRESFFORDD
MEDI 22AIN 1934
IN MEMORY
OF THE 266 MINERS
WHO LOST THEIR LIVES
IN THE
GRESFORD COLLIERY DISASTER
22ND SEPTEMBER 1934

Overleaf: **80.** *Erddig Park, winter*
The River Clywedog flowing through Erddig Park just below Felin Puleston.

Left: **81.** *Little Erddig*
Spring on the Erddig estate.

Below left: **82.** *'Cup-and-Saucer', Erddig Park*
The Black Brook flows into a man-made disc and falls through a central hole creating a cylindrical waterfall before flowing out through a classical bridge-style arch. As well as being fascinating to watch, this unusual feature of Erddig Park has a highly practical and environmentally friendly purpose. It is a hydraulic water ram which uses the artificially created force of gravity to pump water up to Erddig Hall which is sited on the ridge above.

Facing: ***83.*** *Erddig Hall, West Front*
This neo-classical frontage, designed by James Wyatt, was added to the original seventeenth century house by Philip Yorke in the 1770s. This was the main entrance to the house and carriages arrived from Wrexham via Erddig Road and then up the slope from the Clywedog Valley.

Facing: **84.** *Erddig Hall, East Front*
Long spring shadows fall across the garden and ornamental pond at Erddig.

The central block (roughly identified by the higher roof line) was built for Joshua Edisbury in the 1680s. The two side wings were added in c.1721 when the house was the property of John Mellor. The house passed to Simon Yorke in 1767 and remained in that family's hands until it was given to the National Trust by Simon Yorke in 1973. The house had been very seriously affected by mining subsidence and a major restoration programme during the 1970s saved it for the future. The gardens have been recreated in the style of the eighteenth century and are also the home of the national ivy collection.

Right: **85.** *Marchwiel*
Sandstone cottages on the main Wrexham–Whitchurch road at Marchwiel with the tower of St Deiniol & St Marcella's Church in the background.

Left: **86.** *Parish Church of St Deiniol & St Marcella, Marchwiel*
The parish of Marchwiel comprises of two townships, Marchwiel and Sontley. The church was rebuilt in 1778, and the tower (designed by James Wyatt) was added the following year. The building was enlarged in 1829. Inside, there are some fine memorials to members of the Yorke family of Erddig.

Right: **87.** *The Bridge, Bangor-is-y-Coed*
Dating from 1658, this bridge spans the River Dee and links the old counties of Flintshire and Denbighshire. All the land east of the river was in the detached part of Flintshire known as Maelor Saesneg (English Maelor), the area of Maelor closest to England. To the west was Maelor Cymraeg (Welsh Maelor). Both areas are now part of Wrexham County Borough.

When the railway came to Bangor-is-y-Coed in the late nineteenth century, the station was named Bangor-on-Dee in order to differentiate it from Bangor (Gwynedd) and it was felt that the Welsh name was too complicated for the railway passengers.

Left: **88.** *Parish Church of St Dunawd, Bangor-is-y-Coed*
The Welsh word 'bangor' means a monastery or the land enclosed by a wattled fence. In the sixth century, a Celtic monastery stood somewhere near this spot which was reputed to have had 2,000 monks. Following the Battle of Chester in 615 AD, the monks were massacred by Ethelfrith, King of Northumbria, and the monastery was destroyed. Those monks who managed to escape found refuge in Gwynedd where they founded a new monastery at Bangor. Most of the present-day church was built in the 1720s.

Right: **89.** *The Plassey, Eyton*
Completely re-built as a model farm in 1902, The Plassey is now a popular leisure and holiday park situated on the gentle hills above the River Dee.

Above: **90.** *Yew Trees, Overton*
One of the famed 'Seven Wonders of Wales', some yew trees in the churchyard at Overton are believed to be over 2,000 years old.

Facing: **91.** *Overton Bridge*
Another bridge which linked the old counties of Flintshire and Denbighshire over the River Dee. It was built in the early nineteenth cenury by Thomas Penson (junior) and John Carline after a previous single-arched bridge (designed by Thomas Penson senior) had collapsed in 1815.

Above right: **92.** *Cottage, Wrexham Road, Overton*

Overleaf: **93.** *Dispensary Row, Overton*
A fine example of early nineteenth century, brick-built cottages with Gothic style windows.

DISPENSARY
ROW
DISPENSARY ROW

Overleaf: **93.** *Erbistock*
Once the site of a ferry across the Riv
Dee, the picturesque hamlet of Erbistc
is now the location of St Hilary's Churc
(re-built in 1860–1) and the popular
eighteenth-century Boat Inn.

Left: **94**. *Parish Church of St Deiniol, Worthenbury*
Sited just above the flood plain of the
River Dee, and possibly the finest
example of a Georgian church in Wale
St Deiniol's was rebuilt in the 1730s an
is a Grade I listed building. Inside, it
retains its eighteenth century box pew
and several memorial features to the
Puleston family of nearby Emral Hall.

Above and right: **95 & 96**. *Madras V. A. School, Penley*
Founded in 1811, this school was run on the system of 'mutual instruction' first used by Rev. Andrew Bell in Madras, India. Under this monitorial system, one child was taught the basic elements of a subject and he then went on to teach others. The school is highly unusual in being of a cottage design with a thatched roof.

Overleaf: **97.** *Hanmer*

Overleaf: **98.** *Parish Church of St Chad, Hanmer*
Built in the late Perpendicular style, this church is best remembered as the scene of the marriage of Owain Glyndwr and Margaret, daughter of Sir David Hanmer. The church was enhanced in the eighteenth century and restored in 1884 only to be almost totally destroyed by fire in 1889 when little more than the outer walls and the tower survived.

The Vicarage, seen on the left, dates from the early eighteenth century. The poet, R. S. Thomas, was a curate here in his early days as a clergyman.

Left: **99.** *Wynnstay Hall, Ruabon*
Originally called Watstay, this estate was the seat of the Williams Wynn family, probably Wales' largest landowners. An earlier neo-classical house was destroyed by fire in 1858 and the present French Renaissance style house was designed by Benjamin Ferrey. The house became Lindisfarne College in the 1950s and was sold to private developers in the 1990s who converted it into apartments. Many of the more interesting features of the estate buildings have survived including the Chapel, the Dairy (which incorporates a Doric temple) and the Stable Block. The garden, designed by Capability Brown, is Grade I listed.

Facing: **100.** *Wynnstay, Ruabon*
The view of Wynnstay Hall and part of the walled estate from the A483.

Facing: **101, 102, 103 & 104.** *Ruabon houses*
The village of Ruabon grew up around the Parish Church of St Mary and the Wynnstay Estate. Its major claim to fame, however, came in the nineteenth century due to the production of high-quality red bricks. Founded by Henry Dennis in 1878, to utilise the large local deposits of Etruria Marl clay, the Red Works quickly became the largest of its kind. As well as producing the bricks, which soon became known internationally as Ruabon Bricks, the works specialised in the manufacture of quarry tiles and ornamental terracotta which have been exported all over the world. Despite this, the village contains numerous examples of buildings constructed from the local bricks as well as those that pre-date this and use other traditional materials such as sandstone.
From top left, clockwise:
101. Cottages off Church Street.
102. Old Ruabon Grammar School.
103. Cottages, Park Street.
104. Alms Houses.

Right: **105.** *Newbridge Viaduct, Cefn Bychan*
Often forgotten because of its close proximity to the more famous Pontcysyllte Aqueduct, the Newbridge Railway Viaduct is one of the industrial marvels of Wales. Built in 1846–8 by the local railway engineer Henry Robertson to carry the Shrewsbury and Chester Railway across the valley 150 feet above the River Dee, it has nineteen slender arches.

Located below the viaduct is the Ty Mawr Country Park.

Overleaf: **106.** *The Dee Valley from Garth*
This area of the River Dee should perhaps be as well-known for its bridges as for its stunning scenery. In this photograph landscape, flora and bridges are combined in an extraordinary view. Looking east through the densely wooded valley of the Dee, the bridges are the Pontcysyllte Aqueduct, the Newbridge Railway Viaduct and the modern Dee Viaduct carrying the A483 Trunk Road.

Overleaf: **107.** *Pontcsyllte*

This photograph of the old Pontcysyllte Bridge is taken from the Pontcysyllte Aqueduct. This packhorse bridge bears the date 1697 although it is likely that a bridge has stood on this site since earlier times. In the background is an old watermill in which can clearly be seen the old mill race emerging from under the building which once housed the under-shot water wheel.

Left and facing: **108 & 109.** *Pontcysyllte Aqueduct*

Thomas Telford's masterpiece carries the Llangollen canal in a 1,007 feet long cast-iron trough, 127 feet above the River Dee. Begun in 1795, it took ten years to complete and consists of nineteen 45 ft spans. Eac pier is of solid masonry up to seventy feet above the ground and hollow from that point up the the arch. Each joint between the trough sections was made watertight by means of a seal made from Welsh tweed coated in grease. The tow path, originally designed to allow horses to pull the narrow boats across, now provides an exciting footpath for anyone not suffering from vertigo. A plaque on one fo the piers reads: 'Th nobility and gentry of the adjacent counties having united their efforts with the great commercial interest o this country in creating an intercourse and union between England and North Wales. By navigable communication of the three rivers – Severn, Dee and Mersey, for the mutual benefit of agriculture and trade, caused the first stone of the aqueduct of Pontcysyllte to be laid, on the 25th July, 1795, when Richarc Myddleton, M.P., of Chirk, one of the original patrons of the Ellesmere Canal was Lord of the Manor and in the reign of our sovereign George III. When the Equity of the laws and security of property promoted the general welfare of the Nation, while the arts and sciences flourished by his patronage, and the conduct of civil life was improved by his example.'

The aqueduct is currently under consideration as a World Heritage Site.

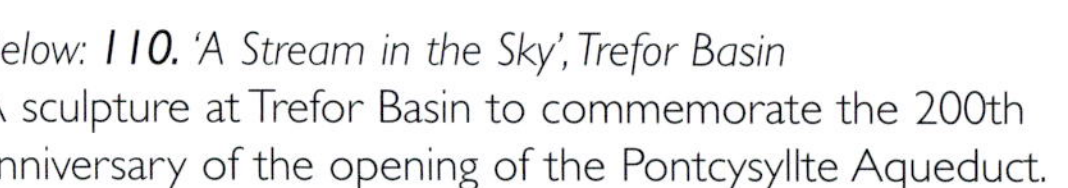

Below: ***110.*** *'A Stream in the Sky', Trefor Basin*

A sculpture at Trefor Basin to commemorate the 200th anniversary of the opening of the Pontcysyllte Aqueduct.

Facing: ***113.*** *Trefor Basin, Acrefair*
Brightly decorated narrow boats moored at Trefor Basin on the northern side of the Pontcysyllte Aqueduct. The public house on the quayside is named after Scotsman, Thomas Telford, the 'founding father' of British civil engineering, who designed and built not only the aqueduct but the canal, the old London–Holyhead Road, the Menai and Conwy Suspension Bridges and many other projects throughout Britain.

Above and right: ***111 & 112.*** *The Llangollen Canal*
Two views of the canal between the southern end of the Pontsysyllte Aqueduct and Chirk.

TELFORD
RESTAURANT * BAR MEALS * COFFEE
FUNCTION ROOM * CHILDREN WELCOME
Scotch Hall
MOORING FOR
PUMP OUT
AND FUEL
← ONLY →
AQUEDUCT

Facing: **114.** *Chirk Castle*
Located on a prominent position between the valleys of the Rivers Ceiriog and Dee, work on Chirk Castle was started by Roger Mortimer in the late thirteenth century to a design by Master James of St George (chief architect of the castles of King Edward I). The castle became the seat of the Myddelton family in 1595 when it was bought by Sir Thomas Myddelton, one of the founders of the East India Company and Lord Mayor of London. In 1978, the Myddelton family handed over the castle to the Welsh Office who passed it on to the National Trust.

Right: **115.** *Chirk Castle Gates, Chirk*
Designed and made by the Davies Brothers of Croesfoel Smithy in 1712, these gates originally stood in front of the castle and were moved to their present location at the main entrance in 1888.

Facing: **116.** *Castle Road, Chirk*
The picturesque village centre of Chirk contains many houses and other buildings of architectural and historic interest including these brick-built cottages on the road leading to the Ceiriog Valley. The former girls' school (now used as a discount warehouse) was designed by renowned architect Augustus Pugin as an additional commission whilst he was working on renovations at Chirk Castle.

Right: **117.** *Hand Terrace, Chirk*
An example of a cottage, built in the neo-Gothic style for the Chirk Castle estate in the early nineteenth century.

Left: **118.** *War Memorial, Chirk*
This often overlooked war memorial was commissioned by Lord Howard de Walden from the artist and sculptor Eric Gill in 1919. The typeface used in this book is Gill Sans, designed by Gill in the 1920s.

Left and facing: **119 & 120.** *Chirk Aqueduct and Viaduct*

The aqueduct was built by Thomas Telford and William Jessop between 1796 and 1801 and, although geographically close to that of Pontcysyllte, it is quite different in design, being composed of ten masonry arches with no cast-iron trough. The canal is 70 feet above the River Ceiriog.

The viaduct, like that at Newbridge (see photographs 105 and 106) was built by Henry Robertson for the Shrewsbury and Chester Railway between 1846 and 1848. Comprising ten arches, the stone viaduct was originally approached (at both ends) by timber gantries which were replaced by six further stone arches in 1858–9.

Left:: **121.** *Ceiriog Valley*
South from the Dee Valley the landscape of the County Borough changes dramatically with the start of the Berwyn Mountains bisected by the beautiful and lush Ceiriog Valley. This photograph shows the northern (or lower) part of the valley looking towards Dolywern.

Right: **122.** *Pandy, Ceiriog Valley*
This hamlet, located just above the former slate quarrying village of Glyn Ceiriog, is named after the buidling on the left which was once a *pandy* or fulling mill. From this point the valley narrows as the road climbs up towards Llanarmon Dyffryn Ceiriog.

Facing: **123.** *Ceiriog Valley, summer*
The upper reaches of the Ceiriog Valley approaching the highest point in Wrexham County Borough. The densely wooded valley further north is now giving way to open pasture and an almost treeless ridge. The economy of this area was historically dependent upon sheep farming.

Above: **124.** *Llanarmon Dyffryn Ceiriog*
The West Arms in the village of Llanarmon Dyffryn Ceiriog (Llanarmon DC for short) close to the head of the Ceiriog Valley.

Left: **125.** *Llanarmon Dyffryn Ceiriog, spring*

PLAS MWYNWYR RHOS

Facing: **126.** *The Stiwt, Rhosllannerchrugog*

Once claiming to be the largest village in Wales, Rhosllannerchrugog was a key coal mining and brick making community until late in the twentieth century. The Miners Institute (The Stiwt) in Broad Street was built in the 1920s to a baroque design by John Owen and F. A. Roberts. It has served the local community as a theatre, cinema, dance hall, social club, billiard and snooker club and meeting rooms until 1977 when it closed. Bought by Wrexham Maelor Borough Council, all attempts to revive the building failed and it was scheduled for demolition in 1985. Strong local feelings eventually led to the reversal of the closure plans and it underwent a major refurbishment in the 1990s turning it into an arts and performance centre.

Right: **127.** *Jerusalem Chapel, Rhosllannerchrugog*

Built in 1770 and enlarged in 1837 (before the major exploitation by the brick industry of the local clay deposits) this stone-built chapel, known locally as 'Capel Mawr', continues to play a significant role in the religious and cultural life of Rhos.

Left: **128.** *Market Street, Rhosllannerchrugog*

The influence of the local brick industry (most likely the Copi Brickworks located just outside the village) is clearly evident in the majority of the village's buildings. Rhos has produced a seemingly endless stream of schoolteachers, ministers, politicians and musicians who have influenced communities not only throughout Wales but much further afield. Among the most notable names are: I. D. Hooson (poet); Arwel Hughes (musician); Meredith Edwards (actor); Tom Ellis (politician); James Idwal Jones (politician) and Thomas William Jones – Lord Maelor (politician).

Overleaf: **129.** *Pentrebychan, Esclusham*

Once the grounds of Pentrebychan Hall, the home of the Meredith family, this rural idyll is now the grounds of Wrexham Crematorium. The house was demolished in 1962 and only the dovecote and walled garden remain.

Overleaf: **130.** *St Andrew's Mission Church, Wern*
Reminiscent of a church on the American frontier, this corrugated iron chapel serves the Anglican community of Wern. 'Tin' churches such as this were mass-produced during the nineteenth century and sold through mail order catalogues to congregations all over the world. Initially, these buildings were intended to serve for only a short time until either they were replaced by a more permanent building or until the need for them declined. Many, like this church at Wern, have survived beyond their purchasers wildest dreams and still perform their original function. Another excellent example can be seen at the Methodist Chapel in Rhosnesni Lane, Wrexham.

Left: **131.** *The Nant, Coedpoeth*
The ford and footbridge across the River Clywedog in the Nant below Coedpoeth.

Facing: **132.** *City Mine Shaft, Minera*
The City Shaft of the Minera lead mine was the deepest in north-east Wales, reaching a depth of 1,220 feet. The engine-house, built in the mid-nineteenth century held a 40-inch pumping engine which operated until 1909. The shaft is now part of the Minera Lead Mines Museum and is an ideal place to start a walk along the 5.5 mile Clywedog Trail.

Above and facing: **133.** *Minera Moors, late summer*
Once past the village of Minera, the valley of the Clywedog gives way to open moorland which displays different colours and moods according to the season. Here, close to the western boundary of Wrexham County Borough, are to be found spectacular views westwards towards the Clwydians and Snowdonia.

Facing: **134.** *Esclusham Mountain, late summer*
Looking west towards Moel Garegog.

Above: **135**, *Wrexham from Minera Mountain*

South Cheshire Plain
The Maelor
Shropshire
Coedpoeth
Wrexham Industrial Estate
Wrexham

Above: **136.** *Minera Moors, mid winter*

Facing: **137.** *Penrhos Engine House, Brymbo*
Built by the eighteenth century iron master John Wilkinson to pump water out of a coal mine, Penrhos is believed to be the oldest surviving colliery engine house in Wales. Today, there are few remaining traces of the industry that occupied this landscape and the stone building has acquired a romantic air.

Above: **138.** *Coedpoeth from the Nant*
The former industrial village of Coedpoeth acquires a new image when viewed from the west across the valley of the River Clywedog.

Overleaf: 139. *Caeau Weir, Bersham*
The River Clywedog flows over the stepped weir as it enters the village of Bersham where its water was a major source of power for the ironworks of the Wilkinson family. The mill race flows through a leat from the top right of the weir, through the woods, to the mill building in the village.

Above and left: 140. *The Bridge at Nant Mill,*
Part of the Clywedog Trail, the path on the right follows the River Clywedog down to the village of Bersham, crossing Offa's Dyke en route

Above: 141. *Bersham*
The centre of the old village with Plas Power Estate cottages dating from the 1850s on the left and beyond (in white) the Accounts House of the Wilkinson Iron Works. On the right is the iron works mill building which is complete with an overshot waterwheel. Later used as a corn mill, it now houses the Bersham Iron Works Museum.

Right: **142.** *St Mary's Plas Power Private Chapel, Bersham*
This fine Romanesque church was built in 1873 as the estate church for Thomas Lloyd Fitzhugh of Plas Power. Still in the ownership of the Fitzhugh family, the church is what is known as a 'Peculiar' and is administered by trust but comes under the Wrexham Deanery of the Diocese of St Asaph.

Overleaf: **143.** *Alyn Waters Country Park, Gwersyllt*
The largest country park in the County Borough, Alyn Waters was developed on former industrial land and the grounds of Gwersyllt Hall, on either side of the River Alyn.

Right: **144.** Lake at *Moss Valley Country Park*
Wrexham's first project to turn a derelict industrial area into a country park occurred at Moss Valley. Here, on land previously occupied by the Westminster Colliery and numerous railway lines, extensive clearing and replanting took place during the 1970s. Today the valley is a rural haven with woodland walks, lakes, a golf course and open countryside within two miles of Wrexham's town centre.

Overleaf: **145.** *Moss Valley Country Park, autumn*
A woodland walk along what was once an industrial railway line in Pentre Broughton.